BESHLIE'S
COUNTRYSIDE

To Marjorie Clark and Carol Blundell

Published in association with

The National Trust
36 Queen Anne's Gate, London SW1 9AS

Text and illustrations copyright © Beshlie 1982, 1988
First published in Great Britain in 1988 by
ORCHARD BOOKS
10 Golden Square, London W1R 3AF
Orchard Books Australia
14 Mars Road, Lane Cove NSW 2066
Orchard Books Canada
20 Torbay Road, Markham, Ontario 23P 1G6
Published in association with Gallery Five
121 King Street, Hammersmith, London W6 9JG
1 85213 045 8
Typeset in Great Britain by P4 Graphics
Printed in Great Britain by Purnell Book Production

BESHLIE'S COUNTRYSIDE

THE BOOK OF

The Harvesters, Milkman & Hop-Pickers

ORCHARD BOOKS

in association with The National Trust
London

Short-tailed Bank Voles
Corn Marigold   Common Red Poppy
Corn Mint   Fluellen
Little Tiger Blue

8

The Harvesters

A few simple tools, but many willing hands were needed for the late summer harvesting of cereal crops. The farmer's family and his neighbours hurried to get the harvest in while the fine weather lasted.

The reaper used a lightweight curved knife called a hook. Such *sickles* were used by the Egyptians. In one hand he held a forked stick which held back the corn ears. This was called a *tharle* and is still used today with a grass-hook. Both are being used in the main picture.

9

Women tied the corn into sheaves with twisted straw rope, standing them into little stooks. These were placed carefully from south to north, for maximum sun, in wide rows so that the horse and haywain could drive through and collect them.

A heavier *bagging-hook* was later invented. This had a wide end which put more force into the reaper's swing, and is still in use in the twentieth century.

The sheaves were tossed onto the wain with wooden pitchforks, and taken to be stored in a barn or made into

early sickle

10

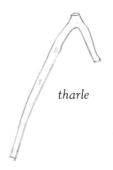

tharle

a rick. During the winter the corn was thrashed, the corn ears beaten off with stick-like implements called flails.

The cornfield was raked with wooden hay-rakes. The farmer's neighbours were allowed to keep any corn they could glean. Gleaning was also done after the ricks had been thrashed, and many poor families lived on the grain they had gathered.

The last waggon-load of sheaves carried the children on top, and often a dolly made of straw. Corn dollies can still be bought in shops.

bagging-hook

calked handle

Common Rock-rose
Daisy   Wood Mouse
Plume Moth

The Milkman

All farms which kept a milk herd had a dairy, however small. Milkmaids milked the cows, often out in the meadows. They then delivered the milk and cream around the villages. It was carried in deep *wooden pails,* hanging by a rope from a *wooden yoke* that fitted on the shoulders.

Milkmen collected milk, cream, butter and cheese from farms on the outskirts of towns. Handcarts were used for delivering. These carried a *large churn* and *hook-handled measures.* Churns were specially shaped,

13

with a wide lip for pouring, a narrow neck so the milk did not spill out and a wide base so that it was not easily knocked over.

Dairies were often under the farmhouse where it was cool. Marble slabs on the dairy shelves kept the milk cold, as there were no refrigerators.

hook-handled measures

churn

14

yoke

Warm milk from the milk pail – there is one by the Milkman in the main picture – was passed through a *straining cloth,* using a measure, into shallow *pans.* When cool, the cream rose to the top and could be skimmed off and churned into butter.

wooden milking pail

15

cooling pan

muslin straining cloth

tiny holes

dished cream skimmer

A barrel churn is shown
in the small picture.
Milkmaids or Dairymaids
churned the cream into
butter and kept the milk
pans clean.

Dairies were established in most large towns and cities. There were many in London which had their own herds of cows.

 deep lid

hand-carrier

The stone or china decoration of a cow's head can still be seen on some old buildings in London, showing that these were once thriving dairies. Barbers had a striped pole outside, dairies had a cowhead.

17

Bank Voles   Hops
Chives   Lucern   Redshanks
Slender Burnished Brass Moth

18

The Hop-Pickers

The rough-surfaced hop vine grows anew each year, twining clockwise up long rods or poles, or nowadays up wires. These were taken down in autumn so that the *yellow cones* which grow on the female plants could be picked, collected in baskets and put into hop-cradles. Both of these are shown in the main picture.

Whole families worked in the hop fields. City dwellers flocked to Kent, Herefordshire, Hampshire, Sussex and Surrey, from July to September, on a profitable working

holiday. Gypsies came in the horse-drawn caravans they call waggons, or on London trolleys — flat-bedded four-wheeled carts — bringing the *bender tents* in which they slept, cooking on a fire on the ground in front of the opening.

The tallyman kept tally, or count, of the number of baskets each family picked, so they could be paid accordingly. He used different shaped *wooden tallies* on a string round his neck as reminders.

wooden tallies

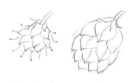

female flower and cone

The damp-loving hop grew wild in Britain long before it was first cultivated, around the sixteenth century.

bender tent

The female cones are the fruit of the hop, and contain resinous glands. These are used to clarify beer. Hops impart a bitter taste, and also act as a preservative.